SHIRLEY,

Nly Gou Dreee

You "DReeH"

To

_____

May God help you
to fill your dash
from this day forward
with His life, hope, and purpose.

from

_____

Published by Word & Spirit Press
Tulsa, Oklahoma USA
http://WandSP.com
e-mail: info@WandSP.com

Printed in the United States of America

ISBN 10: 0-9785352-2-7
ISBN 13: 978-0-9785352-2-3

Author photograph by Matt Harrington Photography, Nashville, TN. Used by permission. Manuscript assistance to author by Joann Klemm

Cover design / Interior design and page composition by Bob Bubnis / BookSetters, Bowling Green, KY

Life in the DASH

a closer look at the not-so-fine line between birth
and what happens next

PHIL GOLDSBERRY

with Mark E. Roberts

WORD & SPIRIT PRESS

Dedication

This book is dedicated to my family, who has made my dash fulfilling and worthwhile:

To my parents: Without you there would be no dash. Thank you for the spiritual heritage and character you poured into my dash.

To Pamela, my unbelievable wife of 30 plus years: Without you the dash would have been empty and unfulfilled.

To my three kids, Danielle, Amanda and Phillip Jr.: You have made the dash valuable and exciting . . . you guys are the best!

To my grandson, Daniel: You have made me want my dash to be long and significant.

To my sons-in-law, Brendon and Christopher: Thank you for loving my girls and giving them a great dash to look forward to.

Contents

See the Dash . .

You've Got Dates!

What Belongs in

What Are You Doing with

The Dash in

. . . . 8

. . . . 20

Your Dash? 29
Your Dash? . . . 52

the Dash 67

SEE THE DASH

Life is a dash between two numbers on a tombstone, and everybody should enjoy that dash.
—Dr. Neil Shulman, inspiration for the movie "Doc Hollywood"

Tombstones don't tell us much. They stand at attention, sentries posted throughout the cemetery. Uniformed in sober gray and black, they command our attention and remind us, with powerful silence, that we too will someday join the throng they guard.

They bear brief testimony to lives lived marvelously long and those so short we may feel moved to tears, even though we didn't know the Garrison baby who lived just 17 days or the Vasquez boy, whose bat and glove, now carved into granite, never felt a baseball after his eleventh birthday.

We see the monuments of the wealthy, as commanding here as their palatial mansions were in life. And we see smaller monuments, headstones, and humble grave markers no larger than a sheet of paper, lying flush with the low-cut grass.

Some gravestones tell us a lot about the lives they mark. The composer of "Amazing Grace," a former slave-ship captain, wrote his own epitaph, which captures the pendulum swing of his life:

JOHN NEWTON
CLERK
ONCE AN INFIDEL AND LIBERTINE
A SERVANT OF SLAVES IN AFRICA,
WAS BY THE RICH MERCY OF OUR LORD
AND SAVIOUR JESUS CHRIST,
PRESERVED, RESTORED, PARDONED,
AND APPOINTED TO PREACH THE FAITH
HE HAD LONG LABOURED TO DESTROY

Other grave markers give us only the barest of facts, found on most markers:

- A first and last name, maybe with a middle initial
- One sentence describing the person's life
- Date of birth
- Date of death

If you're family or a friend of the deceased, every letter and carving on the gravestone may speak to you.

But one little mark found on nearly every grave marker speaks to all of us – *if* we'll see it.

This mark doesn't care whether we know the person whose resting place it marks. Silent, it cries: "See me! Learn my lesson; it's for life!"

Look between the birth date and the death date.

See it?

There, separating a beginning and an ending . . .

BORN—

That little one- or two-inch mark stands for a whole life – everything between birth and death.

In over twenty-five years of pastoral ministry, I've helped with many funerals. In that brief memorial service, it is impossible to recount and relive that little dash. Our feeble attempts seem so minuscule, compared to the grand scheme of anyone's dash. We will read the birth date and the date of passing from this life, and then we attempt to describe and remember the dash – the life lived.

For we the living, of all the information carved so tersely on gravestones, the mute dash is the most important, although it tells us the least: A life was lived, and now this phase of it is over.

But more than what it tells us is what it *urges* us: "Fill your dash wisely!"

All of life is found in that small—but so significant—dash.

Life is in the dash!

DIED

A credit card commercial asks, "What's in your wallet?"

Far better to ask, "What's in your dash?"

Better still, "What's in *my* dash?"

Life is there.

Life: the word exudes hope, challenges, grand possibilities, thrilling opportunities.

All these are in your dash – if you will see it and seize it, while it is holding open the door between your birth and death date.

Most of us have no idea how long our dash will be.

James, the wise man of the New Testament, reminds us of what we don't know:

> YOU DO NOT KNOW WHAT
> WILL HAPPEN TOMORROW!
> YOUR LIFE IS LIKE A MIST.
> YOU CAN SEE IT FOR
> A SHORT TIME,
> BUT THEN IT GOES AWAY.
> — JAMES 4:14 NCV

13

In the cemetery, the dash is frozen in granite,

　　but among the living, it's a vapor:

　　　　here today, gone too soon tomorrow.

We don't know how long any of us have,

　　but we do know that our dash is temporary.

No matter how much or little you've lived,

　　your life is flying by.

　　You can't slow it down.

　　You can't stop it.

At times it seems like things are dragging.

Remember as kids how long it was between birthdays or Christmases?

If you didn't get the gift you really wanted, some well-meaning adult would comfort you: "Just wait for next year!"

Next year? It might as well have been *never!* A year seemed like a forever!

But as adults, haven't you noticed how time really does seem to fly?

My wife Pamela and I are now celebrating more than thirty years of marriage. That seems impossible! It still feels like we are in our late 20's, in some ways (although, at other times, it seems like we're in our 90's!). Our dash together has been amazing. (I tell her that she is like fine cheese: the older she gets, the better. It seems to work!)

It *seems* like our oldest child, Danielle, was just born. But now she has given us our first grandchild. My baby girl is having a baby!

I'm *not* that old! Or am I?

Regardless of how the passing of time feels, our lives are moving on like a mist, a puff of smoke: here, and then gone.

If we are blessed with a "normal" dash, we can expect to journey through seven ages. At least that's what the ancients, the Talmud, and Shakespeare thought about a man's life-span.

The Seven Ages of Man

William Shakespeare

All the world's a stage,
And all the men and women merely players:
They have their exits and their entrances;
And one man in his time plays many parts,
His acts being seven ages. At first the infant,
Mewling and puking in the nurse's arms.
Then the whining school-boy, with his satchel
And shining morning face, creeping like snail
Unwillingly to school. And then the lover,
Sighing like furnace, with a woeful ballad
Made to his mistress' eyebrow. Then a soldier,
Full of strange oaths, and bearded like the pard,
Jealous in honor, sudden and quick in quarrel,

Seeking the bubble reputation
Even in the cannon's mouth. And then the justice,
In fair round belly with good capon lined,
With eyes severe and beard of formal cut,
Full of wise saws and modern instances;
And so he plays his part. The sixth age shifts
Into the lean and slipper'd pantaloon,
With spectacles on nose and pouch on side,
His youthful hose, well saved, a world too wide
For his shrunk shank; and his big manly voice,
Turning again toward childish treble, pipes
And whistles in his sound. Last scene of all,
That ends this strange eventful history,
Is second childishness and mere oblivion,
Sans teeth, sans eyes, sans taste, sans every thing.

— *As You Like It*, Act 2, Scene 7 (c. 1599)

Richard J. Needham puts Shakespeare's eloquence into seven words:

THE SEVEN AGES OF MAN

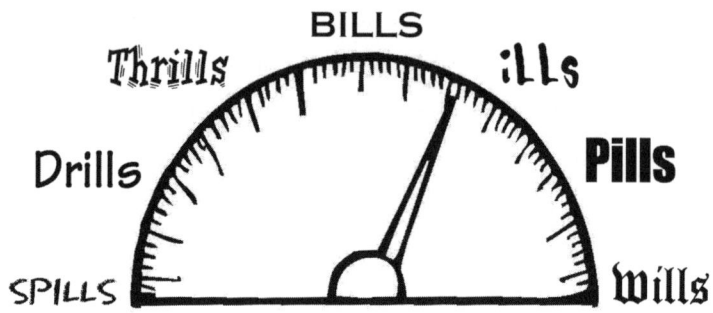

Did you find yourself there?

Think that you have a whole lot of life in front of you?

Maybe so, but do you really know that?

Recently, we lost two incredible young adults – 25 and 35. Two of the finest Christians I have ever known.

On their way to a conference aimed at challenging them and their peers to surrender to world-changing service to the Lord, their dashes ended abruptly.

Neither expected
the crash;
neither expected
the end
of their dash.

YOU'VE GOT DATES!

Before I formed you in the womb, I knew you. . . .
—Jeremiah 1:4

We all know our birth date. Not, of course, because we remember it (although I have heard of siblings trying to have the last word by claiming to remember the color of the room they were born in!).

But our entry into the world of life was a big event for our families. Lots of pain for our moms and lots of surprises for the dads who hang around, supposedly to help. And then, when things have gone well, after perhaps many hours of labor, we arrived!

Mom will soon forget her pain as she bonds with her precious gift. Birth has moved her baby from her womb permanently into her heart.

Mom and Dad together will automatically begin thinking of the future. Not only a baby, but also a dream has been born.

All present—including grandparents and siblings— observe the beginning of a dash.

The Solid Rock

My hope is built on nothing less
Than Jesus' blood and righteousness;
I dare not trust the sweetest frame,
But wholly lean on Jesus' name.

Refrain:
On Christ, the solid Rock, I stand;
All other ground is sinking sand,
All other ground is sinking sand.

When darkness veils His lovely face,
I rest on His unchanging grace;
In every high and stormy gale,
My anchor holds within the veil.

His oath, His covenant, His blood
Support me in the whelming flood;
When all around my soul gives way,
He then is all my hope and stay.

When He shall come with trumpet sound,
Oh, may I then in Him be found;
Dressed in His righteousness alone,
Faultless to stand before the throne.

—Edward Mote (1797–1874)

We all start off the same, wearing the same clothing – *au natural.*

Job said it this way,

> **I was naked when I was born,**
> **and I will be naked when I die.**
> —- Job 1:21 NCV

There were no designer clothes on any of us. You may be a shopaholic now and enjoy the latest in fashion, but when you were born — brace yourself — you were slimy, toothless, and bald (or nearly so).

Yet everyone said you were beautiful and cute – and meant it!

(Fast-forward seventy years, imagine that same head, again bald and toothless. I doubt that "beautiful and cute" are among the words that come to mind!)

In many ways, we were all a blank canvas yet to be painted upon.

We couldn't know what we would be or become.

But we had started: our dash had begun.

We celebrate that day every year, on our "birthday."

Maybe you've had so many of them that you've tried to stop having birthdays. But face it: you're still getting older. Your birthday is going to come around every year, and on that particular birthday, you're going to be one year older.

So we may as well enjoy all those birthday celebrations, especially the big ones – the 18th, the 21st, the 30th, and all those following once-a-decade celebrations.

Even if we wish they wouldn't keep coming, we know when each is coming. If we're having a party, someone looks at that date and plans for it. No question about when its coming. Circle it on the calendar, punch it into your cell phone or PDA years in advance. You know when you were born and when to celebrate each anniversary of your birthday.

But how many of us know our death date?

Once born, our death dates are just as certain as our birth dates.

But unlike our birth dates, we don't know our death dates. You don't know when you're going to die. You don't know when you're going to draw your last breath. But you will draw a last breath.

And then your tombstone will show your birth, which you know, and your death date, which no one but God knows.

You cannot put this appointment in your day planner or calendar. No one says, "Oh, look, look, I'm going to die that day." It's one of the few dates we don't get to set.

Only God knows that date, and we *will* keep His appointment.

Everyone has to die once,
then face the consequences.
— Hebrews 9:27 MESSAGE

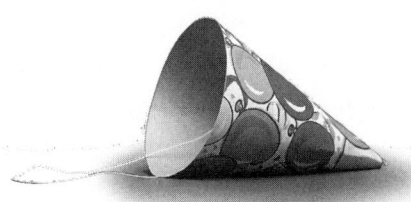

Why discuss death in a book about life?

Because knowing that its date is unpredictable, yet its reality is certain and final, can motivate us to live wisely and well.

Listen to the Preacher of the Old Testament:

> **IT IS BETTER TO GO TO A HOUSE OF MOURNING THAN TO GO TO A HOUSE OF FEASTING,**
> **FOR DEATH IS THE DESTINY OF EVERY MAN;**
> **THE LIVING SHOULD TAKE THIS TO HEART.**
> — ECCLESIASTES 7:2 NIV

By all means feast! Enjoy life! Live to the full!

But first take to heart your destiny. Contemplating death in a right way can help you live better.

Death ends the dash that began at birth, the dash you're in right now.

You've got dates,
and between them
is your dash.
What's going into
your dash?

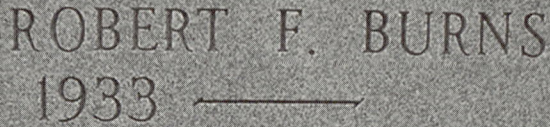

ROBERT F. BURNS
1933 ————

WHAT BELONGS IN YOUR DASH?

PEOPLE ARE OFTEN UNREASONABLE, IRRATIONAL,
AND SELF-CENTERED.
FORGIVE THEM ANYWAY.

IF YOU ARE KIND, PEOPLE MAY ACCUSE YOU OF
SELFISH, ULTERIOR MOTIVES.
BE KIND ANYWAY.

IF YOU ARE SUCCESSFUL, YOU WILL WIN SOME
UNFAITHFUL FRIENDS AND SOME GENUINE
ENEMIES.
SUCCEED ANYWAY.

IF YOU ARE HONEST AND SINCERE, PEOPLE MAY
DECEIVE YOU.
BE HONEST AND SINCERE ANYWAY.

WHAT YOU SPEND YEARS CREATING, OTHERS
COULD DESTROY OVERNIGHT.
CREATE ANYWAY.

IF YOU FIND SERENITY AND HAPPINESS, SOME
MAY BE JEALOUS.
BE HAPPY ANYWAY.

THE GOOD YOU DO TODAY WILL OFTEN BE FOR-
GOTTEN.
DO GOOD ANYWAY.

GIVE THE BEST YOU HAVE, AND IT WILL NEVER BE
ENOUGH.
GIVE YOUR BEST ANYWAY.

IN THE FINAL ANALYSIS, IT IS BETWEEN YOU AND
GOD.
IT WAS NEVER BETWEEN YOU AND THEM ANYWAY.

—ATTRIBUTED TO MOTHER TERESA
(1910–1997)

Several years ago, I began the process of buying a mausoleum for us. The description of our final resting place in that mausoleum sounded wonderful: marble construction set on a beautiful, grassy knoll reached by a tree-lined circle drive. Almost sounded like a Better Homes and Gardens real estate feature. What a way to go!

The director asked, "What do you want to put on it? We'll go ahead and engrave it now. We'll put your name, your wife's name, and your family name. But what is the epitaph that you want to put? We'll go ahead and get that ready too." And guess what?

They were ready to engrave our birth date years followed by a dash. The director said, "We will leave the other part blank, and then we can come out and have that done on site." He deftly avoided the word "death," but that's what "the other part" referred to.

I pondered this. They can engrave nearly everything on there now: names, epitaph, birth dates, and that all-important dash.

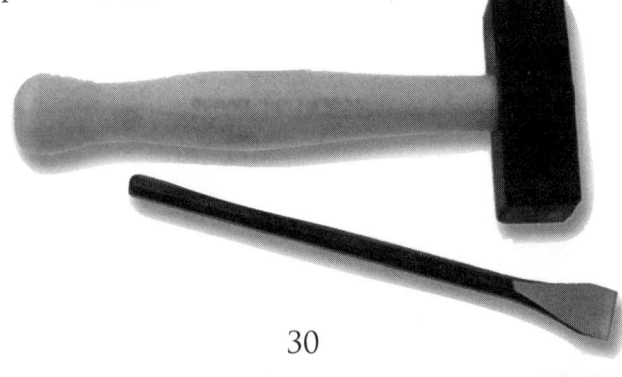

But that's it. The last thing they can engrave now is the dash.

I'm living my dash right now, and so are you.

Because we can't know that last date or when it can be engraved on our gravestone, we are left contemplating the dash.

How are we spending it; how are we filling it?

You might be surprised to know how typical Americans spend theirs.

In an average lifetime, the average American . . .

- is involved in 6 motor vehicle accidents,
- is hospitalized 8 times (men) or 12 times (women)
- catches 304 colds
- makes 1811 trips to McDonalds
- eats 35,138 cookies and 1483 pounds of candy
- consumes 109,354 pounds of food
  and spends . . .
- $89,281 on food
- $6881 in vending machines
- 3 years in business meetings
- 13 years watching TV
- 24 years sleeping.

  — *In an Average Lifetime*,
   by Tom Heymann

Those are interesting statistics, but do they at all correspond to the promise and potential of the generous gift of a full life? Is there anything there you'd want engraved as your epitaph?

Doc Holliday was a Georgia dentist who migrated to the Old West in search of dry climate therapy for his tuberculosis. But we remember him as a hard-drinking gambler and gunfighter who fought alongside Wyatt Earp in the famous shootout at the OK Corral in Tombstone, Arizona.

After a life like that, what would you expect on his tombstone? He didn't write his own epitaph, as you can tell. His tombstone shows his dates – 1852 to 1887 – not a long life, and says, "He died in bed."

What a way to sum up a life! Maybe the point is that none of his enemies filled him with hot lead; but still, wouldn't you want your life to prompt an epitaph-writer to say more than "I died in bed"?

Personal effectiveness expert Stephen Covey has people imagine their epitaph as a part of teaching his second of *Seven Habits of Highly Effective People.* That habit is beginning any endeavor with the end in view. Far from a morbid exercise, drafting candidates for your epitaph has you consider what you want your life to amount to so that your epitaph would fit it.

Whether or not you have arranged or are arranging for your funeral, you have your dash, and you can write your epitaph right now – what you want your life to amount to.

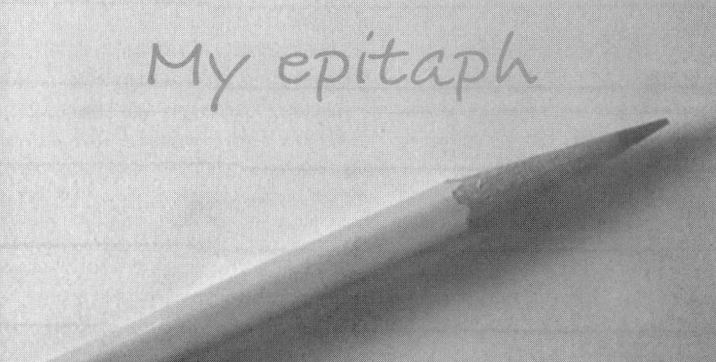

My epitaph

Epitaphs from the Lighter Side

On the 22nd of June
Jonathan Fiddle
Went out of tune

Here lies an Atheist
All dressed up
And no place to go.

Anna Wallace
The children of Israel wanted bread
And the Lord sent them manna;
Old clerk Wallace wanted a wife,
And the devil sent him Anna.

Stranger tread This
ground with gravity.
Dentist Brown
Is filling his last cavity.

Here lies old
Rastus Sominy
Died a-eating hominy
In 1859 anno domini

Here lies the body of our Anna
Done to death by a banana
It wasn't the fruit that laid her low
But the skin of the thing that made her go.

For a hanged sheep stealer in Ireland:
Here lies the body of
Thomas Kemp.
Who lived by wool
and died by hemp.

Come blooming youths, as you pass by,
And on these lines do cast an eye.
As you are now, so once was I;
As I am now, so must you be;
Prepare for death and follow me.

To which someone added:
To follow you
I am not content,
How do I know
Which way you went?

⊳·◄▶·○·◄▶·◄

On Ezekiel Pease:

Pease is not here,   Here lies the father of 29.
Only his pod   He would have had more
He shelled out his Peas   But he didn't have time.
And went to his God

⊳·◄▶·○·◄▶·◄   ⊳·◄▶·○·◄▶·◄

Here lies Pa.
Pa liked wimin.
Ma caught Pa in with two swimmin.
Here lies Pa.

⊳·◄▶·○·◄▶·◄

Jedediah Goodwin
Auctioneer
Born 1828
Going!
Going!!
Gone!!!
1876

⊳·◄▶·○·◄▶·◄

On a hypochondriac's grave:
See. I told you I was SICK!

Reflect:

Seriously, if today loved ones had to order your gravestone, what epitaph do you think they would have engraved on it?

_____

_____

_____

_____

_____

_____

_____

_____

As you think about what your life can add up to, about how you will fill and spend your dash, think about how God intends to fulfill His good and gracious purposes in and through you. Think about what belongs in your dash.

Consider how God expressed a specific purpose for the lives of many in the Bible:

FOR JACOB & ESAU:

AND THE LORD SAID TO HER [REBEKAH]:
"TWO NATIONS ARE IN YOUR WOMB,
TWO PEOPLES SHALL BE SEPARATED FROM
    YOUR BODY;
ONE PEOPLE SHALL BE STRONGER THAN
    THE OTHER,
AND THE OLDER SHALL SERVE THE YOUNGER."

— GENESIS 25:23 NKJV

FOR SAMSON:

AS FOR THE SON YOU [MANOAH AND HIS
    WIFE] WILL CONCEIVE AND BEAR,
NO RAZOR SHALL TOUCH HIS HEAD,
    FOR THIS BOY IS TO BE CONSECRATED TO
    GOD FROM THE WOMB.
IT IS HE WHO WILL BEGIN THE DELIVERANCE
    OF ISRAEL FROM THE POWER OF THE
    PHILISTINES.

— JUDGES 13:5 NAB

To Jeremiah:

For I know well the plans I have in
   mind for you, says the LORD,
plans for your welfare, not for woe!
   plans to give you a future full of hope.

— Jeremiah 29:11 nab

The Psalmist David, addressing God:

You made all the delicate, inner parts
   of my body
and knit me together in my mother's
   womb.
Thank you for making me so wonder-
   fully complex!
Your workmanship is marvelous—how
   well I know it.

— Psalm 139:13-14 nlt

I was thrust upon you at my birth.
   You have been my God from the
   moment I was born.

—Psalm 22:10 nlt

About John the Baptist:

He will be great in the eyes of the Lord.
He must never touch wine or hard
   liquor,
and he will be filled with the Holy
   Spirit, even before his birth.

— Luke 1:15 nlt

38

But, you may be thinking, *I'm not one of those special Bible people. What makes you think that God has some special purpose for me?*

True enough: we shouldn't presume that any specific assignment God gave to them is His assignment for us.

However, God has expressed His purpose for all His people clearly:

WE ARE GOD'S WORKMANSHIP,
CREATED IN CHRIST JESUS TO DO GOOD
    WORKS,
WHICH GOD PREPARED IN ADVANCE FOR US
    TO DO.

— EPHESIANS 2:10 NIV

YOU ARE NO LONGER FOREIGNERS AND
    ALIENS,
BUT FELLOW CITIZENS WITH GOD'S PEOPLE
AND MEMBERS OF GOD'S HOUSEHOLD.

— EPHESIANS 2:19

And God makes it clear that He empowers His people to fulfill His good and gracious purposes with their lives:

> NOW TO HIM WHO IS ABLE TO DO
> IMMEASURABLY MORE THAN ALL WE ASK
> OR IMAGINE,
> ACCORDING TO HIS POWER THAT IS AT
> WORK IN US,
> TO HIM BE GLORY IN THE CHURCH AND IN
> CHRIST JESUS THROUGHOUT ALL GENERA-
> TIONS, FOREVER AND EVER! AMEN.
>
> — EPHESIANS 3:20-21

When the apostle Paul wrote to believers of the church in Philippi, he expressed a confidence that extends to all believers:

> HE WHO BEGAN A GOOD WORK IN YOU WILL
> CARRY IT ON TO COMPLETION UNTIL THE
> DAY OF CHRIST JESUS.
>
> — PHILIPPIANS 1:6

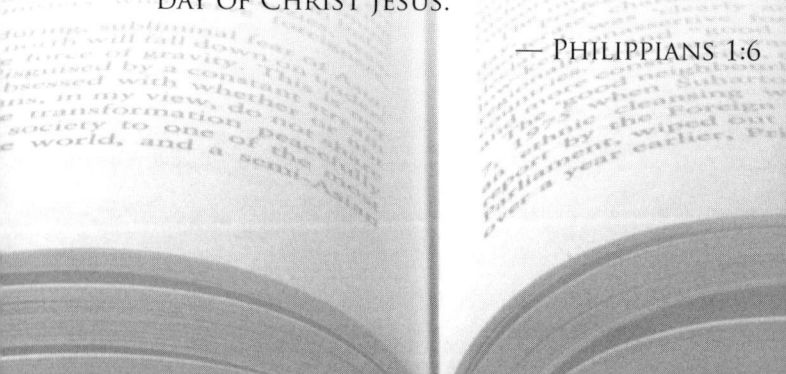

It doesn't matter that you are "not one of those famous Bible people"!

Just as for David, so for you: before you were born, God knew you, knit you together, and destined you. You were born with divine destiny, but a destiny not only has to be given, but it also has to be received.

Are you ready to consider your dash – parts and whole – and to receive God's destiny for you in each area?

Reflect:

Review what you thought loved ones might write for your epitaph. Now here's your chance: If you could live the rest of your life to your highest ideals and fulfill God's purposes for you, what epitaph would then be a fitting tribute when you died? Another way to put this is to say, write an epitaph that fits the life you wish to live intentionally:

_____

_____

_____

_____

_____

_____

_____

_____

_____

_____

_____

Congratulations!

In a creative way, you've expressed something about what you believe to be your life purpose. If you've never before thought about what your life adds up to — and then actually written it down — you've started on the worthy discipline of setting criteria for what belongs in your dash and on what you should spend it.

It goes well beyond the purpose of this book to provide a system for managing your life, including evaluating it regularly and revising as necessary your convictions about your life purpose and how it shows you how to live day by day. (See www.LifeInTheDash.info for inspiration, encouragement, and practical help in living your dash to the full.)

But a life lived well includes regular evaluation and changes along the way. Part of this essential evaluation involves weekly worship with a life-giving church. While worship rightly centers on God, when we worship with others, God's Spirit helps us calibrate our dash, to keep it pointing and leading toward fulfilling His good and gracious purposes for us.

Where else in our world may we gather with people who desire to help us on our way, fellow travelers who focus with us on our Creator and Savior – He who is committed to completing the good work He has already begun in us (Philippians 1:6)?

Don't overlook the valuable resource of the church, the Body of Christ, and the opportunities for worship, friendship, learning, and serving that it provides uniquely.

Encouragement for the Journey

THEREFORE, BROTHERS [AND SISTERS],
   SINCE WE HAVE CONFIDENCE TO ENTER
   THE MOST HOLY PLACE BY THE BLOOD OF
   JESUS,
LET US DRAW NEAR TO GOD WITH A SINCERE
   HEART IN FULL ASSURANCE OF FAITH. . . .
LET US HOLD UNSWERVINGLY TO THE HOPE
   WE PROFESS,
   FOR HE WHO PROMISED IS FAITHFUL.
AND LET US CONSIDER HOW WE MAY SPUR
   ONE ANOTHER ON TOWARD LOVE AND
   GOOD DEEDS.
LET US NOT GIVE UP MEETING TOGETHER,
   AS SOME ARE IN THE HABIT OF DOING,
BUT LET US ENCOURAGE ONE ANOTHER—
   AND ALL THE MORE
   AS YOU SEE THE DAY APPROACHING.

— HEBREWS 10:19-25 NIV

God belongs unquestionably at the center of our lives. And everything we do may and should be worship – even laundry, lawn-mowing, leisure, and love. No part of our lives, no part of our dash, is something secular that God doesn't care about and that doesn't pertain to Him.

As someone has well said, "Not all of life is religious, but all of life is spiritual."

Everything we do matters to God!

We may do everything that is moral and honorable as worship unto God! That is both an amazing privilege – and a sobering responsibility.

So as we consider what belongs in our dash, let us begin with our glorious God and His rightful claim over all of our lives. Radiating outward from His centrality, like spokes from a bicycle hub, are important areas of life that matter to God and that we should consider.

On the next pages, reflect on each area, and write a brief summary of (A) how things are and (B) how you, before God, believe they should be.

Reflection

WHAT BELONGS IN MY DASH?

A. = how things are. B. = how I think they can and should be, with God's help.

1. My relationship with God

    A. _____

    _____

    _____

    B. _____

    _____

    _____

2. Work and relationships with others through work

    A. _____

    _____

    _____

    B. _____

    _____

    _____

3. My specific calling, or vocation (if that differs from my daily work)

    A. _____

      _____

    B. _____

4. Family (including marriage)

    A. _____

      _____

    B. _____

      _____

5. Friends

    A. _____

      _____

    B. _____

      _____

6. Church

    A. _____

      _____

    B. _____

      _____

7. School, or training, and relationships with others

   A. _____

   _____

   B. _____

   _____

8. Finances

   A. _____

   _____

   B. _____

   _____

9. Neighborhood and Community (participation and service)

   A. _____

   _____

   B. _____

   _____

10. Leisure, or recreation, including hobbies

    A. _____

    _____

    B. _____

11. Health, including diet, rest, and exercise

A. _____

_____

B. _____

_____

12. Any other important area:

A. _____

_____

B. _____

_____

If you've reflected and written about most of the above areas, again, Congratulations! You are demonstrating your commitment to receiving your destiny, to maximizing the gift of the dash God has given you.

You may have found some of the blanks difficult to fill in. Perhaps you know that things are "out of whack" in one or more areas. Or perhaps you're not sure "what things can and should be" in some areas. You're not alone. And through your church, help is available. Ask a ministry leader, and he or she will help you or help you find resources that will help.

This section asks "What Belongs in Your Dash?" The simplest answer is this: only those activities that orient your dash toward God, who is the Center, and toward fulfilling His good and gracious purposes for you.

As you can see, at least eleven areas belong in your dash, maybe more. And then, for each of them, specific projects, or activities, belong, because they contribute toward God's wonderful purposes for you and, at the same time, toward your living life to the full. That, by the way, is the reason Jesus came to earth.

A thief comes to steal and kill and destroy, but I came to give life—life in all its fullness.
—John 10:10 NCV

So another way to answer the same question is this: whatever truly advances my dash toward genuine fullness of life, toward receiving God's destiny for me, belongs in my dash.

WHAT ARE YOU DOING WITH YOUR DASH?

> **God,**
> **Please grant me the serenity**
> **to accept the things I cannot change;**
> **the courage to change the things I can;**
> **and the wisdom to know the difference.**
> —Reinhold Niebuhr, 20th-century
> American theologian

Once we've evaluated "the state of our dash" and identified where it can and should go in various areas, we're ready to look at what we are doing in our dash right now.

Is what we're doing helping us receive our divine destiny or pushing it away?

Excuses, blame, and ongoing sin are three ways a lot of people refuse a glorious destiny.

When you looked at various areas of your life, you were probably dissatisfied with where you are in those areas right now. That dissatisfaction may be normal and good—if it prompts us to take responsibility for what we can and, with God's grace, act to improve those areas.

But you also may have found yourself coming up with excuses or blaming others with your dissatisfactions.

We don't control many things:

- the family we were born into

- how we were raised

- whether we were born with a plastic or a silver spoon in our mouth

- whether or not we had a mom and a dad at home

- whether or not our home was religious or Christian

You can add to that list.

We can't change our pedigree. Even if your upbringing was hurtful (and I say this with care), God still knew you and destined your life for glory, for genuine success.

We can acknowledge our past, warts and all, recognize its influence on us, and yet not surrender to the it, as if our past is greater than God!

Nothing is greater than God! And what God decrees or destines for His children, no other force can thwart!

But what about our outright sins?

Do they cripple our dash so that we should not hope for God's favor and the fulfillment of His purposes for our lives?

John 8 tells of scrupulously religious people who attempt to trap Jesus. They catch a couple committing adultery and bring (only!) the woman to Jesus. No question about the act or its category: sin.

Maybe you haven't been caught, but you are committing adultery. Maybe the audit hasn't found it yet, but you are embezzling right now. Maybe no one knows it, but you are hooked on pornography online. Maybe you've hidden your drug or alcohol addiction well; or you've managed to keep shameful acts within your family unknown to outsiders.

If you're honest right now, you're afraid to deal with the truth about your sin, because you're convinced that you've messed up your life so much that there's no hope beyond the shrinking pleasure your sin gives you.

Like you, the woman thinks her dash is over. Jesus, the teacher, maybe even prophet, will surely pronounce God's sentence and allow her accusers to stone her to death.

The accusers push Jesus: "Moses' law says she should be stoned. What do you say?"

Let me paraphrase his response (John 8:7):

> "ALL RIGHT. WE'LL STONE HER. GO AHEAD. BUT THE GUY WHO THROWS FIRST MUST BE SOMEONE WHO IS NOT GUILTY OF ANY SIN."

The accusers demand justice, and Jesus gives it to them. If any of them have sinned but escaped being punished with the strictness they demand to punish this woman, how can they – the guilty-but-unpunished – justly punish the guilty? (And, speaking of justice, why hasn't the adulterous *man* been hauled before Jesus?)

When the accusers hear this, they feel their guilt and slip away, one by one, until only Jesus and the woman remain.

Jesus speaks: "Where are your accusers? Didn't even one of them condemn you?

"No," she answers.

"Neither do I. Go and sin no more."

Own up to your sin.

Don't excuse yourself or blame anyone else.

Confess it, because Jesus says to you, "I don't condemn you. Stop sinning, and live the rest of your dash for the glory of God and the good of your world."

Here's some heavy-duty hope in one of the most wonderful passages of Scripture, which applies to all believers:

WE KNOW THAT GOD CAUSES EVERYTHING TO WORK TOGETHER FOR THE GOOD OF THOSE WHO LOVE GOD AND ARE CALLED ACCORDING TO HIS PURPOSE FOR THEM.

FOR GOD KNEW HIS PEOPLE IN ADVANCE, AND HE CHOSE THEM TO BECOME LIKE HIS SON, SO THAT HIS SON WOULD BE THE FIRSTBORN, WITH MANY BROTHERS AND SISTERS.

AND, HAVING CHOSEN THEM, HE CALLED THEM TO COME TO HIM. AND HE GAVE THEM RIGHT STANDING WITH HIMSELF, AND HE PROMISED THEM HIS GLORY.

WHAT CAN WE SAY ABOUT SUCH WONDERFUL THINGS AS THESE?

IF GOD IS FOR US, WHO CAN EVER BE AGAINST US?

SINCE GOD DID NOT SPARE EVEN HIS OWN
SON BUT GAVE HIM UP FOR US ALL, WON'T
GOD, WHO GAVE US CHRIST, ALSO GIVE US
EVERYTHING ELSE?

WHO DARES ACCUSE US WHOM GOD HAS
CHOSEN FOR HIS OWN?

WILL GOD?

NO! HE IS THE ONE WHO HAS GIVEN US
RIGHT STANDING WITH HIMSELF.

WHO THEN WILL CONDEMN US?

WILL CHRIST JESUS?

NO, FOR HE IS THE ONE WHO DIED FOR US
AND WAS RAISED TO LIFE FOR US AND
IS SITTING AT THE PLACE OF HIGHEST
HONOR NEXT TO GOD, PLEADING FOR US.

CAN ANYTHING EVER SEPARATE US FROM
CHRIST'S LOVE?

DOES IT MEAN HE NO LONGER LOVES US IF WE
HAVE TROUBLE OR CALAMITY, OR ARE PERSE-
CUTED, OR ARE HUNGRY AND COLD OR IN
DANGER OR THREATENED WITH DEATH?

. . . NO, DESPITE ALL THESE THINGS, OVER-
WHELMING VICTORY IS OURS THROUGH
CHRIST, WHO LOVED US.

AND I AM CONVINCED THAT NOTHING CAN EVER SEPARATE US FROM HIS LOVE.

DEATH CAN'T, AND LIFE CAN'T.

THE ANGELS CAN'T, AND THE DEMONS CAN'T.

OUR FEARS FOR TODAY, OUR WORRIES ABOUT TOMORROW, AND EVEN THE POWERS OF HELL CAN'T KEEP GOD'S LOVE AWAY.

WHETHER WE ARE HIGH ABOVE THE SKY OR IN THE DEEPEST OCEAN, NOTHING IN ALL CREATION WILL EVER BE ABLE TO SEPARATE US FROM THE LOVE OF GOD THAT IS REVEALED IN CHRIST JESUS OUR LORD.

—ROMANS 8:28-39 NLT

Wow! With such assurance, we are freed from excuses, blame, and sin that we repent from. We are loved by God, who has destined us to show a family resemblance to our elder brother, Jesus. That heavenly pedigree matters more than our perhaps-blemished earthly pedigree.

And we are freed from weights from the past. Because God loves us and will not abandon us, we are free to confess our sins, to acknowledge our mistakes, and because "he is faithful and just," He "will forgive us our sins and purify us from all unrighteousness" (1 John 1:9 NIV).

We should honestly face, acknowledge, confess, and turn from these, but do not deny God by enlarging our failings so that we give them more power in our lives than we give to God!

Our failures must not anchor us to the past.

With God's forgiveness and love, even our failures can be rudders to direct us into our God-destined future.

Look again at that Scripture passage: "God causes everything to work together for the good of those who love God and are called according to his purpose for them."

Everything – not just fifty per cent or only the good stuff that happens.

No, God, who rules all of His creation, makes everything work for our good. Not everything is good when it happens. We can all say "Amen" to that! But that is not what the Scripture says. It says that God makes all things – including those that began as evil – to work together for the good of His children.

Two Scripture examples help us believe Paul's bold claim.

First, remember Joseph, the dreamer with the multi-colored robe? His story fills the last part of Genesis, chapters 37–50.

Talk about family issues! Joseph was Jacob's late-in-life baby. Daddy doted on Joey, giving him the special robe, which proved to Joseph's eleven other brothers that he was Daddy's favorite. Despite God's choosing of Joseph, he was nevertheless quite a brat.

He's not remembered in the Bible for his pleasing personality. He's remembered in such detail *only because God called him and destined him* to help save his family, the people of Israel.

But before Joseph can save his people, a lot of evil happens to him.

- Jealous brothers sell him to Arabs traveling to Egypt.
- There an official, Potiphar, buys him as a house servant, where his wife tries to seduce good-looking Joseph repeatedly.
- One day his refusal angers her so much that she screams "Rape!" and Joseph goes straight to prison.
- There he helps two servants Pharaoh is punishing. But when one, the cupbearer, is restored to favor, he forgets Joseph.
- That is, until Pharaoh is desperate to find someone to interpret his troubling dreams, and the cupbearer finally remembers Joseph.
- From this moment on, we see Joseph restored, honored, and saving his family from starvation.

Throughout Joseph's ordeal, when undeserved evil hurts him, the Bible shows how God fulfills His calling and destiny, regardless of who or what opposes Him.

- Twice the Bible says "The Lord was with Joseph" (39:2, 21).
- Twice God's blessing on Joseph's work is emphasized: while managing Potiphar's house (39:5) and while managing Egypt (41).
- And twice Joseph assures his brothers that God's good has trumped their evil (45:5-8; 50:19-21). Here's what Joseph said the second time:

> DON'T BE AFRAID. . . . YOU INTENDED TO HARM ME, BUT GOD INTENDED IT FOR GOOD TO ACCOMPLISH WHAT IS NOW BEING DONE, THE SAVING OF MANY LIVES.
>
> —GENESIS 50:19-20 NIV

Second, consider Jesus. For the best example of how God takes evil and turns it to good, read part of what the apostle Peter preached the day God poured out the Holy Spirit:

> JESUS OF NAZARETH WAS A MAN ACCREDITED BY GOD TO YOU BY MIRACLES, WONDERS AND SIGNS, WHICH GOD DID AMONG YOU THROUGH HIM, AS YOU YOURSELVES KNOW.

THIS MAN WAS HANDED OVER TO
YOU BY GOD'S SET PURPOSES AND
FOREKNOWLEDGE; AND YOU, WITH THE
HELP OF WICKED MEN, PUT HIM TO DEATH
BY NAILING HIM TO THE CROSS.

BUT GOD RAISED HIM FROM THE DEAD,
FREEING HIM FROM THE AGONY OF
DEATH. . . . AND WE ARE ALL WITNESSES OF
THIS FACT.

THEREFORE, LET ALL ISRAEL BE ASSURED OF
THIS: GOD HAS MADE THIS JESUS, WHOM
YOU CRUCIFIED, BOTH LORD AND CHRIST.

—ACTS 2:22-24,32,36 NIV

God is the ultimate model of all the superheroes that fill comic books and cinema screens. You think it's amazing that these heroes can intercept meteors, bullets, speeding trains, and deadly missiles, stop them in mid-air, and then hurl them back from where they came?

First of all, they're just fictional characters.

But, second, what they do in make-believe pales before what God has done – and does – in real life.

God took all the evil of humanity, all the contempt for and rebellion against His authority, all of it down to the murder of Jesus on the cross. God took all that we meant for evil, and he transformed it into good.

God took the most vicious form of Roman execution, the cross, and transformed it into the instrument of our salvation!

THE MESSAGE OF THE CROSS IS FOOLISHNESS TO THOSE WHO ARE PERISHING, BUT TO US WHO ARE BEING SAVED IT IS THE POWER OF GOD.

—1 CORINTHIANS 1:18 NKJV

God took our murder of Jesus and transformed it into the sacrifice that covers, or atones for, all the sins of all who trust Him.

CHRIST . . . SUFFERED WHEN HE DIED FOR OUR SINS ONCE FOR ALL TIME. HE NEVER SINNED, BUT HE DIED FOR SINNERS THAT HE MIGHT BRING US HOME SAFELY TO GOD.

—1 PETER 3:18 NLT

> JESUS CHRIST, THE RIGHTEOUS ONE: HE
> IS THE ATONING SACRIFICE FOR OUR SINS,
> AND NOT ONLY FOR OURS BUT ALSO FOR
> THE SINS OF THE WHOLE WORLD.
>
> —1 JOHN 2:2 NIV

God did this for Joseph and through Jesus, and God is faithful, so why can't we dare to believe that God will transform all of the evil, sin, and failure in our lives – both what others have done to us and what we ourselves have done – into good?

This truth is gospel – good news about what God has done and continues to do.

There is no catch, no fine print, only the fact that all these things are true for those who are in a good relationship with God, that is, those who trust and love Him.

So anyone who is continuing to rebel against God should not think that God has promised to cause "all things work together for good for me."

No, the promise is "those who love God and are called according to his purpose for them." Let's elaborate a bit.

What does that mean to "love God?"

> We love sirloin,
>> Starbucks,
>>> the Internet,
>>>> apple pie,
>> and Chevrolets (or Jeeps or Hummers).

But do we truly understand love for the invisible God?

This love is not primarily an emotion
> or a sentiment
>> or a craving by one of our five senses.

All these are involved in loving God, but they are not the essence of this love.

Jesus showed that love for God involves our total being:

LOVE THE LORD YOUR GOD
> WITH ALL YOUR HEART AND
>> WITH ALL YOUR SOUL AND
>>> WITH ALL YOUR STRENGTH AND
>>> WITH ALL YOUR MIND.

—LUKE 10:27 NIV

And he identified the proverbial "proof in the pudding":

> IF YOU LOVE ME, OBEY MY
> COMMANDMENTS.
>
> — JOHN 14:15 NIV

What do heavy words such as "obey" and "commandments" have to do with "love"? Don't they link in our minds to other heavy words we'd rather avoid, words such as "duty" and "obligations," things we have to do whether or not they make us feel good?

We need to learn an old truth that our world has nearly forgotten. It's the truth about "ordinate love" — that is, the love that justly fits the thing that we love.

It's okay to speak of loving fishing or shopping, as long as the loyalty and affection we have for those activities fits their true value.

Obviously love for our spouse and children merits a whole lot more loyalty and affection – even duty and obligation – than love for a day on the lake or new shoes.

If we love fishing, say, or shopping, more than taking care of our children, we would all agree that we love those activities too much. We would love them unjustly, or inordinately. Even good activities become wrong, or evil, for us when we love them more than they deserve to be loved.

Think of all the things – items, activities, and persons – in your world. List a sampling of five of them below:

_____

_____

_____

_____

_____

Now rank them in order, one to five, based on how much love each deserves.

_____

_____

_____

_____

_____

Which deserves the most love? The least?

Where does God go on the list?

Easy answer, right?

Does God deserve more and better love than our careers, our friends, our family, even our earthly lives? Of course He does.

And that is why Jesus says that our love for God must express all that is within us. Anything less is unjust. In fact, when we fail to love God fully, we commit the most basic injustice in the universe, because God *deserves* such love and nothing less.

And He "causes everything to work together for the good of those who love God and are called according to his purpose for them."

And the dash well spent, the life well lived, is all about love – all about loving each thing with the kind of love that is right for it.

What does "called according to his purpose for them" mean?

It really restates what it means to love God. Loving God, because He is the Supreme Being of the universe, means acknowledging His authority and His claim over our life. It means offering for His purposes all that we have and are.

As the apostle Paul puts it,

With eyes wide open to the mercies of God, I beg you, my brothers [and sisters], as an act of intelligent worship, to give him your bodies, as a living sacrifice, consecrated to him and acceptable by him. Don't let the world around you squeeze you into its own mold, but let God remold your minds from within, so that you may prove in practice that the plan of God for you is good, meets all his demands, and moves toward the goal of true maturity.

—ROMANS 12:1-2
PHILLIPS

Have you done that?

Do you give yourself ("bodies" stands for our whole selves) to Him and for His purposes in His world each day?

As we do, we have God's assurance that he will cause our dash to prosper, to flourish, to fulfill His good and gracious purposes for us.

BE VERY CAREFUL HOW YOU LIVE.
DO NOT LIVE LIKE THOSE WHO ARE
NOT WISE,
BUT LIVE WISELY.
USE EVERY CHANCE YOU HAVE FOR
DOING GOOD,
BECAUSE THESE ARE EVIL TIMES.
SO DO NOT BE FOOLISH,
BUT LEARN WHAT THE LORD WANTS
YOU TO DO.

—EPHESIANS 5:15-17 NCV

God will transform your failures into stepping stones if you will embrace His destiny for you. Discern where He's leading, and live your dash with gusto!

THE DASH IN THE DASH

Nothing in the world can take the place of Persistence. Talent will not; nothing is more common than unsuccessful men with talent. Genius will not; unrewarded genius is almost a proverb. Education will not; the world is full of educated derelicts. Persistence and determination alone are omnipotent.
—President Calvin Coolidge (1872–1933)

Completing our dash calls to mind another kind of "dash" – the foot race.

Viewing life like a race is popular in the Bible. The writer of the letter to Hebrew believers puts it this way, after leading us through the Hall of Faith (chapter 11), filled with exemplary believers who lived their dash to the full by faith in God:

> THEREFORE, SINCE WE ARE SURROUNDED BY SUCH A HUGE CROWD OF WITNESSES TO THE LIFE OF FAITH, LET US STRIP OFF EVERY WEIGHT THAT SLOWS US DOWN, ESPECIALLY THE SIN THAT SO EASILY HINDERS OUR PROGRESS.
>
> AND LET US RUN WITH ENDURANCE THE RACE THAT GOD HAS SET BEFORE US. WE DO THIS BY KEEPING OUR EYES ON JESUS,

ON WHOM OUR FAITH DEPENDS FROM
START TO FINISH.

HE WAS WILLING TO DIE A SHAMEFUL DEATH
ON THE CROSS BECAUSE OF THE JOY HE
KNEW WOULD BE HIS AFTERWARD. NOW
HE IS SEATED IN THE PLACE OF HIGHEST
HONOR BESIDE GOD'S THRONE IN HEAVEN.

THINK ABOUT ALL HE ENDURED WHEN SIN-
FUL PEOPLE DID SUCH TERRIBLE THINGS
TO HIM, SO THAT YOU DON'T BECOME
WEARY AND GIVE UP.

—HEBREWS 12:1-3 NLT

The apostle Paul faced the end of his dash and de-
scribed it as a race:

I'M ABOUT TO DIE, MY LIFE AN OFFERING
ON GOD'S ALTAR. THIS IS THE ONLY RACE
WORTH RUNNING. I'VE RUN HARD RIGHT
TO THE FINISH, BELIEVED ALL THE WAY.
ALL THAT'S LEFT NOW IS THE SHOUTING—
GOD'S APPLAUSE! DEPEND ON IT, HE'S AN
HONEST JUDGE.

—2 TIMOTHY 4:6-8 MESSAGE

How can we complete our dash – whether for mere seconds or for decades – so that we finish strong and faithful to God's assignment for us?

Another passage from the apostle Paul may show us the way. In it he dismisses all his old badges of spiritual accomplishment as nothing but rubbish, when contrasted with the glory of knowing, having, and becoming like Christ. Then he continues:

NOT THAT I HAVE ALREADY OBTAINED
ALL THIS, OR HAVE ALREADY BEEN MADE
PERFECT, BUT I PRESS ON TO TAKE HOLD
OF THAT FOR WHICH CHRIST JESUS TOOK
HOLD OF ME. BROTHERS [AND SISTERS], I
DO NOT CONSIDER MYSELF YET TO HAVE
TAKEN HOLD OF IT. BUT ONE THING I
DO: FORGETTING WHAT IS BEHIND AND
STRAINING TOWARD WHAT IS AHEAD, I
PRESS ON TOWARD THE GOAL TO WIN THE
PRIZE FOR WHICH GOD HAS CALLED ME
HEAVENWARD IN CHRIST JESUS.
—PHILIPPIANS 3:12-14 NIV

Completing the dash in our dash boils down to zeroing in on our own "one thing."

First, we commit to God's destiny for us. It may or may not be clear to us at any particular moment in our lives. Some people know their life vocation, their specific calling, early in life and stick to it successfully. If you are one of these, keep on track. We'll cheer you on!

But many of us discern our destiny only over time, through experience, and with divine gifts of guidance. Don't worry if The Meaning of My Life is not clear to you right now. Trust God; seek for His wisdom, His guidance, and be looking and listening for it.

Even when we know our primary vocation in life, we still have to express it through several key roles we fill. If, for example, you know that your destiny is to create art that celebrates God's creation (and earns a living!), you'll still have to coordinate that work with family, finances, life in a community and church, and all the other realities of life today.

Second, as we discern our destiny, we give ourselves fully to God's work through us. The apostle Paul tells believers that

> GOD IS WORKING IN YOU TO HELP YOU
> WANT TO DO AND BE ABLE TO DO WHAT
> PLEASES HIM.
>
> —PHILIPPIANS 2:13 NCV

Good news bulletin: We are not self-created projects! Our Creator-Savior called us into this life and is seeing through His project with us!

As we discern God's leading, we can pour ourselves into His work for us, and our dash overflow. My friend Mark has been finding more clarity about his destiny, his vocation, in his early 50's. He told me, "I edited books for several years while I was a pastor and earning a Ph.D. so I could teach college. I succeeded but without the conviction that '*This* is why I'm on earth.' But recently, I've been able to get friends published and started a publishing company. Work has poured in. I'm being invited to write for other projects and to create reference books. Soon I may have to decide if I will publish fulltime. I won't stop preaching and teaching, but writing and publishing may become my most important work. When I do it, I know that it really pleases God."

My friend is zeroing in on his lifetime's "one thing."

How about you? Don't worry if it's not yet clear. But have you committed your dash to God's destiny? Are you daily seeking what it pleases Him to do with and through you? As you discern your vocation, are you making it your "one thing"?

Remember the eleven life areas we reflected on? To complete our dash well, we also evaluate each continuously to focus on the "one thing" that will bring the most good to each area. Stephen Covey has us imagine an empty jar. Next to it are small piles of sand, gravel, pebbles, and big rocks – but so much that surely we can't fit all into the jar. How do we get the most material into the jar? We load the items in order of decreasing size—large rocks first, then pebbles, then gravel, then sand.

The big rocks are the most important things for each area of our lives. If we take care of them *first*, we will accomplish the most. *The life lived well is the life that consistently takes care of the most important "one thing" for each life area first.*

Covey helps us more with the simple concept of the Four Quadrants of life:

	Urgent got to be done now!	**Not Urgent** easy to postpone
Important **really** **matters,** whenever it's done	**QUADRANT 1** PEBBLES • see dentist for bad toothache • pick up sick child from school • pay overdue bill to save credit rating • add oil to car after warning light stays on	**QUADRANT 2** BIG ROCKS • have dental check-up • enhance marriage & friendships • seek God's direction for family and work • exercise 3x per week • give generously • update will, insurance coverage, retirement plan
Not Important doesn't matter much	**QUADRANT 3** GRAVEL • buy HD big-screen TV to get 0% interest – offer expires today • satisfy chocolate craving • join friends going for coffee instead of meeting job deadline • watch favorite TV serial show	**QUADRANT 4** SAND • window shop – clothes or cars • read pleasure magazine • read junk mail / e-mail • play video games • surf Internet mindlessly

What belongs in your dash?

What are you doing with your dash?

What are you making the dash in your dash?

Go forward with great confidence! Trusting in God's faithfulness to see His work completed in you, *carpe diem!* "Seize the day," and make something out of the rest of your dash!

Say "No!" to excuses, blame, and sins and mistakes in the past. No to "I would, but . . ." or "I could, if only . . . ."

As Zig Ziglar says, "If *ifs* and *buts* were candy and nuts, we'd all have a Merry Christmas!"

Instead, regardless of your circumstances, heed Erma Bombeck's wise wit:

"Seize the moment. Remember all of those women on the Titanic who waved off the dessert cart?"

You can do it. God *will* help.

Ready to dash ahead in your dash now?
On your mark.

Get set.

Ready.

Go!

It is God who is at work within you,
giving you the will and the power
o achieve his purpose.

—Philippians 2:13 phillips

I FEEL SURE THAT THE ONE WHO HAS
BEGUN HIS GOOD WORK IN YOU
WILL GO ON DEVELOPING IT UNTIL THE
DAY OF JESUS CHRIST.

—PHILIPPIANS 1:6

LINK THE DASH

Life in the Dash was written to challenge you to take a close look at where you are now in your dash. None of us knows our end date, but we have this moment right now. Extend the value of this book at our website, which will encourage, challenge, and share in your joy in your life in the dash:

www.LifeintheDash.info

There you will find help as you make decisions about your dash. It offers a simple study that will help you fill your dash with eternal significance and encourage you with valuable insight.

There is also a place to send comments or suggestions. Our goal is to assist as many people as we can to truly find "Life in the Dash."

PHIL GOLDSBERRY

ABOUT THE AUTHOR

Phil Goldsberry has a passion to see people realize God's potential for them in their dash: bringing answers to the searching, possibilities to those stuck in life, assurance to the skeptical and those losing hope, and a firm hope in God's unconditional love and faithfulness to all.

With his wife of over thirty years, Pamela, he has three children – Danielle, Amanda, and Phillip, two sons-in-law, Brendon and Christopher, and one grandson, Daniel. Phil has served, since May 2006, as Senior Pastor at Christ Life Church in Tempe. Previously he and Pamela served on the senior pastoral staff of Christ Church, Nashville, as founding pastors of Solid Rock Ministry, in Long Island, and in various pastoral roles of churches in Indiana and Michigan.

Pastor, communicator, teacher, singer, Phil has dedicated his life to spreading God's good news of life lived to the full in the dash.